PRACTICAL GUIDE 1

The Project Approach

MAKING CURRICULUM COME ALIVE

SYLVIA C. CHARD, PhD

Department of Elementary Education

The University of Alberta

CONTENTS

Introduction

Section I
Reviewing Today's Classroom Practices

Teacher instruction or children's construction? Children need
explicit direction for acquiring skills as well as ways to apply their
knowledge to relevant work.

What classroom techniques best support project work? Teaching
and learning are interactive processes. They take into account
how, when, where, and with whom children should work and learn.

What does a rich learning climate look like?
Creating a provocative and engaging learning environment
requires adjustments and some special provisions. Educators
need to shift roles (and often the physical environment itself)
during the course of project work.

What is a project? What is not a project?
Themes and topics can become the foundation of study for
children. Additionally, there are ways to easily integrate all
of the subject areas and essential learning processes.

Section II
Understanding the Project Approach

What are the different levels of project work?
The Project Approach progresses through a sequence of key
events that provides the framework for curriculum planning.

What do projects look like from the learner's point of view?
Projects provide children with developmentally appropriate
goals while offering teachers a foundation for understanding
children's progress.

What evidence of learning should teachers collect?
What should they do with the information?
Authentic performance assessment and evaluation become
the means to systematically document children's development.

How is a community of collaboration and contribution created?
Learning incorporates not only teachers and children, but the
parents as well. Involving parents in the process and work
allows for the continuity of experience between home and school.

Conclusion

Foreword

Welcome to the first in a continuing series of practical guides to the Project Approach. These guides were developed by Dr. Sylvia Chard to help teachers every step of the way in implementing good projects with children from preschool through the elementary grades.

As can easily be seen in this first guide, the series addresses a wide range of practical issues that teachers confront in planning and conducting projects, and drawing them to a successful close. In addition, many terms are defined, and suggestions for a range of options to use in project work are outlined. The guide is full of vivid examples taken from real classroom life illustrating how parts of a project might go, strategies other teachers have tried, and a variety of specific tips to help you find your own best ways to incorporate projects into your classroom work.

Best wishes,

Lilian G. Katz, PhD
University of Illinois
Urbana-Champaign

Getting the Most From This Book

Research and developments in education have recently led to instructional innovations designed to make the classroom into a learning environment that is more responsive to the varying learning needs and interests of children. In recent years, there has been increasing curriculum integration in order to establish continuity in what children learn in the different subjects. There is more opportunity to relate home and school learning. There is concern for memorable learning as well as memorized learning. In addition, children are now expected to work cooperatively on complex and open-ended tasks as well as learning to follow instructions in step-by-step learning. The project approach provides one way to introduce a wider range of learning opportunities into the classroom.

HOW CAN TEACHERS RESPOND TO INDIVIDUAL LEARNING NEEDS?

Classrooms today contain groups of children with a wide range of individual differences. These differences include various physical, perceptual, and mental disabilities, as well as giftedness in children who need special academic challenges of various kinds. There are also classrooms that are multiage, multiethnic, and multilingual. All these children require attention to their individual needs within the classroom. Many schools no longer practice grade retention. These trends in classrooms are challenging some of the instructional methods that were particularly effective when children in the regular classroom were considered homogeneous groups expected to learn and achieve in similar ways.

There is increasing recognition that children have a much wider range of capabilities than they had usually been permitted to show in the regular classroom. In order to demonstrate these capabilities, however, they need learning environments that are responsive to the many differences in their learning styles. Some children, for example, have a special interest in, and early mastery of, symbol systems. Others understand best through much and varied hands-on manipulative experience. Children learn in different ways, have different styles, and build on very different backgrounds of experience. Children also achieve at a higher level in school if they are interested in what they are doing. Interests can vary considerably within an average class group.

HOW IS THIS GUIDE ORGANIZED?

This guide is designed to offer teachers and school administrators a rationale for the Project Approach, a description of the practical implications of its implementation, and ways of integrating parts of the approach with other ways of teaching. Teaching through projects was first written about in *Engaging Children's Minds: The Project Approach* by Lilian Katz and Sylvia Chard. The Project Approach is not a new approach but a restatement of ideas that have been important throughout the history of education. This guide is divided into two sections. Each section presents key concepts to explore:

❶ Reviewing Today's Classroom Practices
This section examines issues as they relate to children and learning. Each topic addresses an important aspect of education.
The Learner An account of children's learning is given that can form a useful basis for planning and evaluating progress.
The Instruction Effective teaching and classroom management techniques are presented.
The Learning Environment Examines the teacher's role in managing an environment where a variety of different activities are in progress.
The Content A detailed comparison between topics and theme, units and projects, and a step-by-step approach to creating a project topic with children.

❷ Understanding the Project Approach

This section describes the Project Approach through a series of topics.

Phases of Project Work A walk-through of the three phases of project work. An outline of what each phase has to offer and how the phases differ from one another is given.

Children's Work: Processes and Products This section gives a detailed description of children at work on projects.

Evaluation and Assessment A distinction is made between the kinds of learning that can be assessed in the different parts of the programs.

The Roles of Teachers, Students, and Parents A look at how parents can be better informed about their children's learning and more involved in their progress both in school and at home.

Research has suggested that change is most meaningful and effective when teachers are actively involved in developing alternative ways of working with children. This guide attempts to make the practical details of the Project Approach easily understandable so that you can try some of the suggestions and evaluate the outcomes.

A CASE STUDY EXAMPLE: THE RAIN STORE

In one classroom the kindergarten and first-grade children are working in groups and on their own, in different parts of the classroom, and in the yard just outside. In the corner of the room is a dramatic-play area, which has been set up as a store. The children have made a big sign that says, "THE RAIN STORE." Two of them are arranging raincoats, hats, boots, and umbrellas on hangers and shelves. Another child is discussing prices with a "cashier" at the little checkout counter.

By the window in the room, one child is writing a poem about the rain that fell earlier in the day. She has first made a list of rain words: *falling, drops, pattering, windows, gray, puddles.* Three children are painting pictures of rainy scenes. Two others are drawing chalk lines around puddles in the yard and measuring the distance across the puddles in various directions. The puddles are drying up, and at half-hour intervals these children draw new chalk lines to record the evaporation rate of the water during the morning. They also draw the puddles' decreasing circumferences on paper so that they

A "project" is defined here as an in-depth study of a topic or theme.

can tell the other children about their work at the class meeting at the end of the morning.

The teacher is working with six children at a table in the middle of the classroom. Jars, bowls, elastic bands, pitchers of water, and several different kinds of material and fabric sit on the table. The children are experimenting to see which materials let the water through faster and which materials seem to be the most waterproof. The teacher encourages close observation of the effect of the water on the fabrics. One child is writing down the words being used to describe what is happening. Another child has predicted that the water would best be kept out by very thick fabric. Testing that hypothesis leads to the further study of absorbency. Someone investigates in a larger bowl how the more absorbent fabrics behave when squeezed and immersed in the water. The children are fascinated by the way the water is soaked up by a thick, woolly mitten.

Several books on rain, water, and the weather have been borrowed from the library. A group of children sitting in the book area read to one another from the books and discuss what they are reading about. On a table nearby lies an umbrella. Four children are drawing the umbrella with pencils and felt-tip pens.

Before the children leave the room for lunch at the end of the morning, they review the work they have been doing. One child tells of the book he read; another talks about events in "the rain store." One of the group involved in the science activities with the teacher tells of their findings. The children measuring the shrinking puddles in the yard talk about their drawings. Later in the day there will be time for further review and for the story the teacher plans to read about a family caught in a rainstorm while having a picnic by a lake.

Note: The description of this classroom gives an idea of what a class project looks like in full operation. From this account many possibilities for teaching and learning can be inferred and many questions raised. In the ensuing pages of this guide I shall offer detailed information about how a teacher can work this way with children for at least part of the time in any classroom.

Reviewing Today's Classroom Practices

Teachers themselves must learn in the way that the children in their classes will be learning.

Eleanor Duckworth

"The Having of Wonderful Ideas"
and Other Essays on Teaching and Learning

The Learner

A balanced curriculum takes into account the various modes of instruction and the many different needs of children. In some parts of the curriculum children are necessarily dependent on the teacher, and in others they can work more independently. There are two aspects of the curriculum that provide for children's learning needs in important ways:

- systematic instruction for the *acquisition of skills*

- project work for the *application of skills* acquired earlier

WHAT IS THE ROLE OF PROJECT WORK?

Children not only need to know *how* to use a skill but also *when* to use it. They need to learn to recognize for themselves the contexts in which the skill might be useful and the purposes it can most appropriately serve. Project work and systematic instruction can be seen as providing complementary learning opportunities. In systematic instruction the children acquire the skills, and in project work they apply those skills in meaningful contexts. The project work can be seen as the part of the curriculum that is planned in negotiation with the children and that supports and extends the more formal and teacher-directed instructional elements.

Some distinctions between systematic instruction and project work

SYSTEMATIC INSTRUCTION	PROJECT WORK
For acquiring skills	For applying skills
Activity at instructional level	Activity at independent level
Teacher directs child's work	Teacher guides the child's work
Child follows instructions	Child chooses from alternatives
Extrinsic motivation	Intrinsic motivation
Addresses child's needs	Builds on child's strengths

When a teacher is instructing a child in a new level of skill, the learning tasks have to be carefully matched to the child's abilities. When children are applying skills in which they have some fluency, they can work independently and with more confidence, make decisions, and solve problems as they arise.

Distinctions Between Systematic Instruction and Project Work Project work takes into account children's questions and curiosities about the world around them. The types of activity the teacher plans will vary according to the desired goals. The teacher's role is different in relation to the child's needs. When children are acquiring skills, the teacher is more of a director. When children are applying skills they already have, the teacher is more of a guide. The child also feels quite different about the activity according to which kind of learning is involved.

	SYSTEMATIC INSTRUCTION FOR ACQUIRING SKILLS	PROJECT WORK FOR APPLYING SKILLS
Examples	telling the time making bar graphs designing experiments	investigating change doing a survey and representing the results investigating water pollution
Activity	unknown, new challenging required closed, limited steps	familiar (in a new context) intrinsically satisfying chosen exploratory, open-ended
Teacher	instructs prescribes directs encourages effort	gives guidance suggests alternatives observes, listens, questions encourages ideas
Child	is as yet incapable follows instructions acts with help is uncertain about ability accepts teacher's evaluation works alone	is capable, proficient practices skills unaided acts independently is confident about ability judges own success often consults, collaborates

WHAT SHOULD CHILDREN LEARN?

In making important decisions about children's learning goals, it's important to ensure that the curriculum reflects consideration of the following: knowledge, skills, dispositions, and feelings. Traditional education already emphasizes goals for the acquisition of knowledge and skills. But teachers have always noted the importance of developing children's confidence in their strengths and their willingness to pursue their own ideas, elements of disposition, and feelings. Coordinating these goals along with knowledge and skills is an important part of project work.

Knowledge

There are many social and scientific concepts fundamental to our way of life that children can learn in the classroom. These have been well documented in curriculum guides and school textbooks. Knowledge also takes the form of stories, personal anecdotes, myths, songs, poems, and other such works.

- **Information:** facts, cultural perspectives, stories, works of art

- **Concepts:** schemas, event scripts, attributes, categories

- **Relations:** cause and effect, how objects and processes relate, part-whole

- **Meaning:** personal experience of knowledge, individual understanding

Skills

Skills are relatively small, clearly defined, observable units of behavior or action. In addition to learning many basic skills and how to apply them, children need to acquire social and personal skills. The learning environment of the classroom offers opportunities for applying skills that promote collaboration.

- **Basic academic skills:** talking, reading, writing, counting, measuring

- **Scientific & technical skills:** data management, use of computers and scientific equipment, observation

- **Social skills:** cooperation, discussion, debate, negotiation, teamwork

- **Personal relationships:** give and take, appreciation, assertiveness

Dispositions

Dispositions are habits of mind or patterns of behavior. Children need to develop certain dispositions to enable them to be effective learners. For example, teachers can develop children's disposition to be interested in their work, thereby facilitating learning and energizing effort. As children's disposition to try out alternatives in their work is strengthened, they can learn to evaluate their own achievement and learn from mistakes or errors of judgment. Those dispositions that are dysfunctional for learning can be weakened or discouraged; for example, the disposition to solve social problems with aggressive behavior or to give up trying when work gets difficult.

- **Habits of mind:** wondering, figuring out, predicting, explaining, and so on

- **Approaches to work:** challenge-seeking, persistence, reflection, openness

- **Preferences:** cooperating/alone, longer/shorter, time, active/passive

- **Strengthening & weakening:** promoting useful dispositions and discouraging dysfunctional ones

Feelings

The way children feel about their work is important for achievement. In project work the challenge of some learning may result in unpredictable feelings of elation or disappointment as children become absorbed in tasks that they have helped to design for themselves. As children take more ownership of their work they also have to learn appropriate emotional responses to success and failure in themselves and in others. Evaluation involves recognizing personal strengths and limitations, and working on them with courage and determination. As children feel increasingly competent and sense their own potential for learning, they develop feelings of confidence and self-esteem. Resulting benefits include:

Project work calls upon the teacher's ability to build on children's natural inclination to enjoy becoming absorbed in their work.

- Setting realistic expectations for achievement

- Coping with frustration, disappointment; appreciating success

- Appropriate expression of feelings and seeking support when needed

- Recognizing moods, crises, blocks as potential obstacles to learning

- Dealing with success and failure, learning from errors of judgment

- Finding ways to deal with personal problems

HOW CAN SCHOOLS HELP DEVELOP POSITIVE SELF-ESTEEM?

An optimum level of self-esteem has been associated with achievement. On the one hand, self-esteem is learned in a social context. On the other, self-esteem grows from the sense of accomplishment people feel as they form, strive for, and realize personal life goals.

The climate of a classroom is important for appropriate self-esteem in relation to learning. Children can best develop self-esteem in a climate where individual differences are appreciated. They benefit when the teacher sets clear expectations of classroom work, behavior, and relationships. They are also helped when the teacher and the other children appreciate their positive contributions to classroom life and learning.

Competition with others for standard outcomes can be discouraging for many children and therefore not helpful to them in their learning. In project work children can compete in seeking divergent or alternative outcomes without such discouragement because the possibilities allow for alternative responses at many levels. Opportunities can be provided for children to contribute in original and creative ways. In classrooms where children are encouraged to evaluate their own achievement, they develop a healthy sense of competition with their own earlier performance rather than with other children.

A SENSE OF PURPOSE IN THE CLASSROOM

Negotiating the curriculum with children help builds a sense of inclusion and investment.

A child's disposition to work in a classroom is strengthened by a corporate sense of purpose. In systematic instruction it is usually necessary for the purpose of the work to be the responsibility of the teacher. The teacher assesses what is required based on her understanding of what the children do not yet know, what they cannot yet do, and what might be the best means of helping them to acquire the necessary skills and understandings. The teacher directs the children's work according to her judgment of their learning needs. In project work, however, the teacher looks at the children from a different perspective. She sees them in terms of their individual strengths, of what they can already do and how they might use, for their own purposes, the skills they have already acquired.

The children can assume some responsibility for the kinds of work they undertake in project activities. For example, the teacher can let them decide on the level of challenge they feel confident with, the length of time they plan to take, the level of detail or elaboration that might be appropriate for them, whether they wish to work alone or with another child. Making these choices allows children to take ownership of some of the work and accept responsibility for the amount of effort and quality of the ideas they bring to the activity and for any product that results.

In a classroom where the teacher can monitor choices, the children can offer rich explanations of how and why they undertook the activities as they did. The teacher can remain in communication with the children throughout the activity by requesting reports from time to time or by intervening in the activity from the sidelines, as appropriate. The teacher's role in project work is that of a guide and consultant in enabling the children to practice and apply their skills to the best of their ability.

Children who are used to a climate for learning such as the one described here exhibit considerable intrinsic motivation to negotiate possibilities with the teacher in their own work. Where the teacher encourages such an approach to learning, the social culture that develops in the classroom is that of a community of learners — teacher and children.

THE CLASSROOM ENVIRONMENT

Teaching and learning are interactive processes. These processes are facilitated in classrooms with particular kinds of organization. The next two chapters provide suggestions about the kinds of classroom environments that most effectively support the Project Approach.

The Instruction

> What classroom techniques best support project work? Teaching and learning are interactive processes. They take into account how, when, where, and with whom children should work and learn.

Project work thrives on children's intrinsic motivation. One of the most powerful motivators for children in the classroom is *choice*. When children can make a choice from among a range of authentic alternatives and can choose when, for how long, where, and with whom to work, their motivation is likely to be greatly enhanced.

WHAT IS THE ROLE OF GROUP INSTRUCTION?

One of the roles of educators is to help provoke and respond to different learning discourses. This calls for a more flexible approach to instruction.

Small Group Instruction The teacher can plan her day so that she spends a good deal of the time instructing children in small groups (4–12 children). While one group is being instructed, the rest of the class can be doing project work. Group instruction is economical. The instruction can be focused, and individual children's misunderstandings can be recognized and corrected straight away. Ten or fifteen minutes of intensive instruction is usually enough. The children working independently can be taught not to interrupt the teacher (except in an emergency) during this period. The children in the instructional group can then be involved in follow-up tasks. This allows the teacher to move around the room to monitor the project work as well as continuing to supervise the instruction follow-up. Then after a few minutes, another group can be assembled for instruction. Where a teacher favors whole class instruction for half the day, there will be less need for small group instruction during the time of the day planned for project work.

Whole Class Discussion It is a good idea early in each day to have a whole class meeting when the children can be informed or reminded of the range of project activities they can choose from. A list of these can be posted for children to refer to easily at any time. They may also have additional practice tasks to undertake following instructional sessions. Many aspects of project work can extend over several days for many children. Individuals and groups can share and discuss their ongoing work in the whole class meetings.

HOW SHOULD THE CLASSROOM STRUCTURE SUPPORT INSTRUCTION?

When to Work Most schools have some scheduling around the availability of the gym or library. Apart from this, teachers can leave the day open as much as possible so children can plan their own work schedules. The work would include certain requirements specified by the teacher. These may include some writing, some drawing, and some math activity every day in relation to the project. Most children can manage their time well with some help.

Where to Work Space in the classroom may also leave room for some choice and decision-making among the children. Some space will be dedicated to particular activities, but other space may be freely available for any work for which no special equipment or resources are needed, such as drawing, reading, or writing. Here too, the teacher can help the children decide for themselves by alerting them to the advantages and disadvantages of different kinds of space for different kinds of work: Enclosed space is good for individual work, round or hexagonal tables are good for cooperative work, etc. The availability of a variety of furniture and a functionally varied layout facilitate such decision-making.

Remember — teachers are learners as well! How does an educator's curiosity influence children's learning?

With Whom to Work Children can also make responsible choices about whom they would like to work with. Sometimes, however, the teacher decides in order to bring certain children together for particular purposes. Some tasks are best worked on alone, others in pairs, and still others in groups of three or four children working cooperatively.

Child Ownership of Project Work Here the matter of choice concerns the nature of the work to be done. Children can choose from among the range of alternatives the teacher makes available. Children writing a report may decide whether to illustrate it with crayon drawings or watercolor paintings. They can choose the color and size of paper to use. More significant choices may include whether the report should be long or short — a two-page report or a ten-page book. This kind of choice provides a most important benefit: It encourages students to take ownership of what they do in school. They develop pride in their work and enjoy having it appreciated.

Peer Support Children are especially interested in the work of others when it is not work which they themselves have undertaken. They do not like to miss out on a good experience. They also learn to express appreciation for the work of others. The teacher is then not the only source of approval for children. Nor is the teacher the only source of help and advice. Children learn to support one another and discuss problems and alternative solutions.

Intrinsic Motivation and Accountability Intrinsic motivation to do project work can be high because the children are interested in what they are doing and have made choices and decisions about what to do and how to do it. Under these conditions children tend not only to take responsibility for their own work but also to be respectful of the work of others. They are willing and able to explain their thinking and also take more risks in what they do. If they make mistakes or errors of judgment, they know that they will be expected to analyze what happened and learn from it.

The Role of the Teacher As the teacher moves around the classroom monitoring the project work, she acts as a guide and consultant rather than a director of operations. She can watch for opportunities to ask questions that help children think about a range of alternatives.

Flexibility allows educators opportunities to observe teacher-child as well as child-child relationships.

She can make suggestions for consideration, not necessarily for adoption. She is also in a position to redirect children who are engaged in unproductive activity or who are pursuing vain efforts to solve a problem. Often, the teacher can question the children about their intentions in such a way that they find a more appropriate solution themselves. The teacher can guide the children in ways that strengthen their disposition to reflect on the implications of the various strategies they consider.

Reminders or Reprimands There are frequent opportunities during the school day to discuss the work going on. This need not interrupt the flow of events unless the teacher wishes it to. The beginnings and ends of sections of the day and the period just before or after recess or lunch are good times for a whole class meeting. Individual children can talk with the class about what they have been doing, or the teacher can cite an example of a student's work that illustrates her expectations in some way. The teacher might talk about particularly original or ingenious work or about a case where the child has succeeded by persisting in the face of difficulty. Sometimes the teacher uses such an example to point out an effective way of solving a problem. Providing children with examples of a successful strategy is more helpful than reprimanding them for not using one.

HOW CAN THE NEEDS OF ALL CHILDREN BE MET?

Students who are choosing many of the features of the work they are involved in tend to be intrinsically motivated. However, the work does have to be well planned and monitored. Not all children work quietly or with concentration for long periods without teacher assistance. Some children have dispositions and approaches to work in the classroom that make responsible, independent work very difficult for them. Some may have little interest in any school activity. These children may present teachers with difficulty in any kind of classroom.

Children With Learning Difficulties   In a classroom where there is productive project work in progress, there are some special advantages to helping children with learning difficulties or with behavioral or social issues. However, where there are many opportunities for children to make choices, there are also opportunities for errors of judgment. Some children may choose activities that are unproductive to their learning. Success for all children will require the teacher's selective guidance of children who are experiencing difficulty. Other strategies include:

Exploring alternative strategies will allow all children to be successful.

- allowing for a wide range of activities to be engaged in.
- using other children as interesting models for students with difficulties.
- having some children discuss and agree upon their schedules with the teacher rather than choose for themselves.
- encouraging some children to work in a specific location in the classroom.
- allowing children to work alone during given times.

Restricting Choices: Constraint and the Power of Self-Determination

These management techniques for restricting the amount of choice for some children work well in the classroom. If a student cannot manage time, the teacher takes over. This can also happen with choice of space and/or choice of collaborator. The power of such a classroom environment lies in the rewards and satisfactions awaiting children with difficulties: the freedom to choose their own work, time, location, and partners. These children make strong efforts to take the required responsibility in order to gain a measure of self-determination. The constraint of children with problems is a matter for constant negotiation between teacher and students.

The Learning Environment

What does a rich learning climate look like? Creating a provocative and engaging learning environment requires adjustments and some special provisions. Educators need to shift roles (and often the physical environment itself) during the course of project work.

The teacher is very influential in setting the climate of the classroom community. The climate has various aspects. The social aspect reflects the kinds of social interaction experienced among community members. The teacher can teach social values conducive to learning and set clear expectations for children's behavior towards one another. She can make sure that individual rights are protected, including those of minority groups. In this way, the children also develop the expectations of their teacher.

Appreciation of and respect for others can be shown in various ways. The classroom is a place where people can share fulfilling experiences as a community of learners if needs and concerns are appropriately expressed and problems discussed. Support, encouragement, and models can be provided by both teacher and peers. Where expectations for children's learning are high, it is important that the social interaction itself facilitate learning. The following are some notes on issues and principles to be considered by the teacher who would like to develop projects:

- Quality of school life (risk-free environment, shared responsibility, etc.)
- Rules, very few, negotiated for safety
- Rights, protection, class community, individual rights, minority groups
- Routines (cleaning up, being economical, helping others)
- Support and reminders (notices in strategic places, atmosphere of coaching)
- Shared expectations (clearly set, challenging, exemplary)
- Sense of purpose (shared group, individual child's, teacher's, agreed, respected)
- Infrastructure (flexible, responsive, developed as time progresses)
- Management (flexibility, the teacher is an authority, organizer, facilitator, collaborator, advisor, consultant, arbitrator, monitor, and delegator)
- Accountability (choice, decision-making, initiative, ownership, responsibility, record-keeping)
- Culture (social values, respect, appreciation, cooperation, negotiation)

THE CLASSROOM AS A LEARNING ENVIRONMENT

Another aspect of the classroom climate concerns the way the space is used. Where there are to be different kinds of learning activity in progress at any one time there has to be provision for quiet thoughtful writing, independent reading, math activities requiring the use of manipulatives, collaborative tasks, artwork with paint or clay, model construction, and group instruction. At times the teacher will want to talk with the whole class at the same time. This works best with the children sitting on a carpet in a small area of the room, as the proximity makes it easier for the children to participate in the group discussion.

Arranging the Physical Spaces The walls and horizontal surfaces can be used to display information, reference lists of relevant or frequently used words, children's work products, suggestions for work procedures, and reminders about routines and responsibilities. Displays can also include real-world objects for close study, information books to consult, aids to observation such as magnifiers, and examples of techniques the children might like to try in their own work.

"Stimulating and validating"...two ideas to consider when creating the learning space.

Another feature of the spatial organization of the room concerns materials the children need to use in their work. If children are allowed to help themselves, they must first be offered criteria for making appropriate choices and encouraged to be economical and tidy in the use of resources. A basic checklist of considerations would include:

- **Space:** appropriate provision of areas for various kinds of work
- **Furniture layout:** flexible, for group as well as individual work
- **Display:** walls, horizontal surfaces, for information, children's work products, work in progress, objects of interest, notices, instructions, word lists, reminders, plans
- **Resources:** convenient access, availability, restrictions, storage
- **Finished work:** work products of various kinds can be put in agreed convenient places where the teacher can check them
- **Children as monitors:** enlist children's help in managing the space, work areas, resources

QUALITY TIME IN THE CLASSROOM

The teacher can help the children to make the most valuable use of time by offering them realistic choices and by setting clear expectations. Individual children vary greatly in the ways they prefer to use their time for work. Some children can concentrate for long periods on the same piece of work; others work best if they can change their activity every few minutes. Concentration may vary from one kind of activity to another. One child may prefer to spend a long time in investigative activity, another in dramatic play, another in reading, and yet another in observational drawing. Preferences may be quite short-lived in some children and remarkably stable and persistent in others.

There is a great deal of flexibility possible in the management of time in a classroom, by both teacher and children. The teacher can ask all the children to work for a given period on a particular task, or she may require a fixed period of time for a particular group of children only. The teacher can also vary the periods of time within which an activity might be offered as a choice. For example, he might require one task to be completed by all children within half a morning whereas another activity might be available as a choice across several days. The responsibility of the teacher is to plan what seems to be most appropriate for the children in the class at the time. This may well change as the school year progresses. Time management is an important feature of the classroom climate and offers considerable potential as an area of serious negotiation among children and between teacher and child. Some time management issues to consider are:

- **Fixed or flexible:** children need help with predicting and managing their own use of time
- **Pace:** more/less time needed, affected by interest, energy, type of work
- **Frequency:** as children need and like to repeat tasks/activities
- **Quality:** consider the needs of the children
- **Negotiated:** teacher needs to monitor, advise, decide after negotiation
- **Time allowance:** to do by end of morning, in two days, or across a whole week
- **Stages:** is the work to be developed over a period of time progressing through several stages? (Different stages require different amounts of time.)

RESOURCES IN THE CLASSROOM

The classroom can be supplied with a variety of resources. Not all of these need be expensive. Some can be collected for temporary use in particular projects and stored for use by other groups. Parents may lend items of special interest for a project.

When children are working independently, applying skills that they already have, it is important to have supplies of paper, paint, clay, model-making materials, construction sets, math equipment, basic science equipment, dramatic play resources, a classroom library in a reading area; for the youngest children, sand and water tables; and for the older children, easy access to good encyclopedias. Whole class sets of textbooks are not needed for project work.

Sources of Information for Work on Projects   Children can acquire information from two types of sources: primary and secondary sources. There are five main kinds of primary sources of information: people, places, real objects, events, and processes. Secondary sources include books, posters, magazines, videos, libraries, and museums.

Fieldwork outside the classroom is a primary source that can provide children with much firsthand information they can use in project activities. Sometimes it is possible for all the children to go on a field trip; at other times they can go in small groups. When the field site is nearby, the children may make several return visits. Children can also go on interesting visits with their parents outside school time and report to the class through their independent fieldwork.

Primary sources: learning directly from their own and another person's firsthand experience

- Firsthand experience of children and teacher in the class
- Firsthand evidence gained on a field trip
- Explanations and guidance from an expert at the site of a visit
- Interviewing an expert visiting the classroom

Secondary sources: learning indirectly from material organized or presented by others

- Information acquired by children through research out of school time
- School library, resource room, other teachers
- Books, brochures, films, videos, etc.
- Museums
- Local community library

All these sources can contribute to the study of a topic in the classroom. Younger children can grasp primary source material more easily, and it contributes greatly to the vitality of the project work in the lower grades.

The Content

Many different kinds of things may be studied. The topic may be concrete or abstract in nature, local or distant, present-day or historical, small or large scale. The younger the children, the more concrete, local, present-day, and small scale the topic should be in order to enable them to draw on their own prior understanding. The fullest understanding is based on relevant, firsthand, interactive experience.

WHAT IS THE RELATIONSHIP BETWEEN TOPICS AND THEMES?

A topic might be trivial or important; it may suggest an infinite range of content — from amoeba to elephant, sand to volcano, cooking to religion, life to death. It can be a starting point for discussion that will eventually range more widely.

The word *theme* suggests a more abstract idea such as "transportation," or "justice." It implies a more planned or crafted progression, such as in the notion of developing a theme. It suggests an overarching, general concept that connects several ideas. In the educational context, *theme* often suggests didactic intent on the part of the teacher.

A Case in Point It is useful to take a closer look at the distinction using an example. Consider the topic of food. Food is within everyone's daily experience. As such, it is topical — it has a here-and-now quality. When we are hungry, we want food.

In the school context we frequently find the corresponding area of study to be the theme of nutrition. Nutrition is more of a theme because it contains the notions of how man understands the nature of food, food that is good or bad for us, food that is used by the body in different ways, food that is digested in different ways by different parts of the digestive tract, and so on.

What is a project? What is not a project? Themes and topics can become the foundation of study for children. Additionally, there are ways to easily integrate all of the subject areas and essential learning processes.

The younger the children, the more important it is that a project be the study of a topic rather than a theme. Young children's own experiential starting point for the study will be "food," not "nutrition."

Of course, no project on food would omit consideration of nutrition. But it would be considered a main idea that emerges from the study of the topic of food, rather than the starting point of the study. With older children, who have more formal background knowledge, however, it may well be more appropriate to begin a study from a more abstract point of departure.

More on Definitions To take the definition of terms one step further: The word *theme* or *topic* should be thought of as the subject of study rather than the study itself. A project involves planning, then implementing and elaborating plans. It involves eventually bringing a study to a conclusion in the achievement of a set of agreed goals. These goals will have been developed in detail during the course of the work rather than specified in advance.

WHAT IS THE DISTINCTION BETWEEN A UNIT AND A PROJECT?

The word *project* might then be more comparable in its meaning to the word *unit* than to *topic* or *theme*. There are, however, some differences between a project and what is frequently understood by the term *unit*.

A project develops more organically than a unit. A unit tends to be pre-planned in greater detail by the teacher, who sets the goals without negotiating with the children. A unit plan often compels all the children to undertake the same work, whereas a project is planned to offer choices to children and may involve them in very different kinds of activity from one another. A project often continues for a longer period of time than a unit.

Criteria for Topic Selection Not all topics are equally promising in terms of their educational potential. Deciding on the criteria to use in choosing a topic of study depends on how children learn best, the basic social values we expect children to live by, and what we understand the role of the school to be in educating children. The following is a set of criteria in the form of questions that can be asked about the value of a topic.

How can a study of this topic...

- build on what children already know?
- help children to make better sense of the world they live in?
- help children to understand one another better?
- enable children to understand the value of literacy and numeracy in real-life contexts?
- offer children ideas for dramatic play/representation?
- encourage children to seek sources of information outside school?
- facilitate communication with parents?

WHERE SHOULD PLANNING START?

Once the teacher has decided on the topic of the project it is important to do some planning before the work begins in the classroom. This planning consists of the following: making a topic web, making an outline of key events, investigating possibilities for fieldwork, and then collecting basic resources.

Topic Webs Making a topic web enables the teacher to use his or her general knowledge of the topic as a starting point for planning the project. People have very similar but slightly differently organized mind maps of any topic. When the teacher starts with her own mind map or web, she becomes more interested in the topic and curious about her own knowledge. She can also more easily evaluate the ideas the children offer and incorporate them into the planning.

The teacher can incorporate younger children's ideas into the web as they arise in class discussion. Older students can make their own topic webs using similar techniques to those suggested here for the teacher.

Topic webs help teachers anticipate when curriculum might naturally emerge.

They can then compare them with those of other students. The teacher and the whole class can work together on one large topic web over the first few days of the project. The web is a useful tool in planning but need not be fixed in its final form in the early days: It can be modified and elaborated as the work progresses.

As the project develops, a chart paper version of the web may be posted and used to record the activities completed and areas of particular interest. The items that have not yet been covered can be noted and then discussed so that children are aware of further options. Some key events, objects or equipment that might be borrowed for classroom study, and possible visiting experts can be noted on the web. Different-colored pens can be used for the different weeks, and dates can be added so that the web provides an ongoing record of the project.

The teacher can keep her own copy of the web, note the achievements of individual children or groups, and record evaluations of the work as it progresses. (Older children can refer to an enlarged version posted on the classroom wall).

How to make a topic web

If a teacher is inexperienced at making topic webs, here is a good way to begin. This activity may be undertaken by a group of teachers at the same time, each working individually. The resulting web can be shared and discussed. If teachers are working in a team on the same topic, webs can be combined in the process of planning a project.

Materials (per person)
▲ 1 pad of the smallest size sticky notes
   (1 1/2" x 2", 100 in the pad)
▲ pencil
▲ paper (8 1/2" x 11")
▲ large clear space on a table

Time
about 45 minutes to 1 hour (depending on number of people)

Procedure
❶ Brainstorm Individually, write as many words as you can that relate in any way to the topic, one word on each sticky note. The words should be as specific and concrete as possible. (Time: about 7 minutes)

Tips
- Use visual imagery.
- Think with reference to all your senses.
- Think about people whose work is involved with this topic.
- Resist the temptation to think of abstract categories.
- Spread the notes on the table as you go.
- Continue for about 7 minutes or until you have about 50 or 60 notes.
- Work alone at this stage even if you are planning to team-teach.

❷ Sort Sort the words into groups of items that are alike and items that are different from other items. When you do this, you may find you have very different numbers of items in the groups. (Time: about 5 minutes)

Tips
- Break down very large groups into subgroups.
- If you have a group that has only one or two words in it, see if you can think of some other words that would belong.

(The aim is not to get groups of equal size but to understand the attributes that particularly characterize each group.)

❸ Label Write headings, or category labels, for each group. Choose the word or short phrase that best expresses the concept connecting the items. (Time: about 5 minutes)

Tips
- You may find you want to regroup one or two sets of items during this process.

- You can, of course, add any new ideas that occur to you.
- You may discover that one of the words in a group is the one you wish to have as the heading for the whole set.
- It is helpful for clarity to make the headings look different, by using a different-colored paper or pen.

4 Share If you are doing this activity together with other teachers, now is the time to look at what other people have done in their webs.

Tips

- Note the common features: Some items and categories will appear in all the sets.
- Some items will be specific to one set and may reveal special interests or experiences a person has.
- As you look at each other's work, make note of any ideas you would like to incorporate into your own web.

The idea is not to make the webs identical but to take advantage of one another's best ideas. This sharing is the kind of collaboration that characterizes useful teamwork.

5 Transcribe The final task is to transcribe the groups of words onto one sheet of paper in web format. This format is preferable to any kind of flowchart because the ideas are represented not in sequential order but as a constellation radiating out from a central idea, the topic or theme title.

Tips

- Write the title of the topic in the center of the paper (circle).
- Surround it with the group headings (underlined).
- List the items in each group outward from the headings.

Any group heading can generate subcategories. See examples in the webs on the following pages.

The topic webs can be used to plan and record the work as the project develops. Older children can refer to an enlarged version posted on the classroom wall.

Weather Topic Web

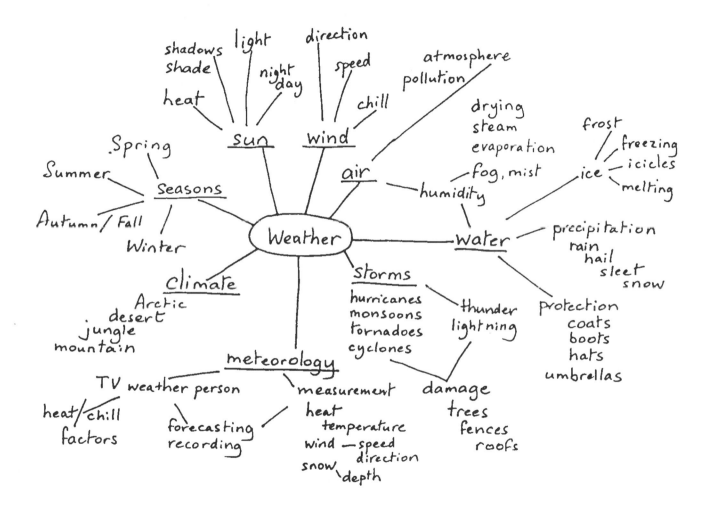

Construction Site Topic Web

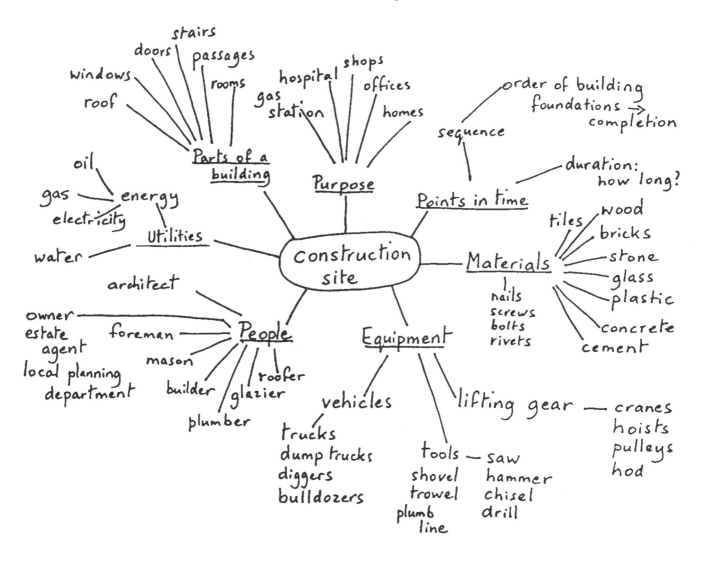

Understanding the Project Approach

Worthwhile experiences, both within the planned learning environment and in the wider community, are never narrow. There are always numerous ways in which experiences and events can develop.

Cathy Nutbrown

Threads of Thinking:
Young Children Learning and the Role of Early Education

Phases of Project Work

Projects develop through three phases. Like a good story, the project can be described as having a beginning, a middle, and an end, each memorable in its own way. In each phase the teacher has particular concerns for children's learning. When the teacher's and children's expectations for a phase have been met, the project proceeds to the next phase; this process continues until the work is concluded.

Phase 1 At the beginning of the project, the teacher's role is to find out how much individual children already know and what firsthand experiences form the basis of their current understanding. The children engage in an initial discussion of the topic and offer ideas and stories of their experiences. They also paint, draw, write about, dramatize, or role-play the experiences and understandings they bring to the study. The children acquire a collective baseline understanding of the topic through representing their own experience and sharing their work in class. A letter is sent home to parents informing them of the topic of study and inviting them to offer any expertise they may be able to share with the class. Throughout the first phase questions are collected for later research. The first phase concludes with the list of questions the children would like to investigate.

Phase 2 The next phase of the project involves planning fieldwork and inviting experts to the classroom to talk with the children. The teacher's concerns center on the provision of new firsthand experiences for the children and the collection of other resources. A field trip is arranged. Real objects and processes are investigated, questions answered, more questions posed, explanations sought. Children read, write, draw, compute, gather data, and represent many different kinds of findings and reactions to their experiences. A representative selection of the work is displayed on walls and shelves for all the class to see.

Phase 3 The final phase culminates in presenting and sharing the project work in some form with others — the principal, other classes, and parents. The work is reviewed and evaluated, and particular items are selected for the presentation. The emphasis is on the communication of learning. There are also opportunities for children to personalize the new information for themselves in more imaginative art and dramatic activity and in personal story and poetry writing.

HOW LONG IS EACH PHASE?

Phase 2 takes more time than either Phase 1 or Phase 3. With the younger children, proportionately more time should be spent on Phases 1 and 3 than with the older ones. The table shown indicates very approximate proportions and refers to whole class projects.

		PHASES		
		1	**2**	**3**
G R A D E	**K**	25%	50%	25%
	3	20%	60%	20%
	6	15%	70%	15%

Suggested time frames

WHAT ARE THE KEY EVENTS OF EACH PHASE?

In each of the three phases there are key events that help to shape the project. They form the basic framework around which the rest of the project can be developed. These events can be recorded on the original planning web by the teacher or on a class web posted for children to refer to.

Phase 1 ~ Starting the Project

Initial Starting Point The opening event stimulates interest for the whole class. This may consist of a personal experience (shared by the teacher or children), a story, a video, or the presentation of an unusual object for the children to pass around, examine, and speculate about.

Topic Web Plan With older children it can be interesting to collect ideas from the whole class and map out what they already know about the topic from their own experience. Some children can make individual topic webs.

Listing Questions It can be helpful for the children to collect questions they would like to investigate in the course of the project. The questions can be recorded on a posted list or put into a box; in either method, questions can be added as they arise. At the end of Phase 1, the questions can be reviewed and discussed.

Phase 2 ~ Investigation and Representation

Preparation for the Fieldwork One or more field trips can be arranged for which there needs to be some preparation. In preparation for fieldwork, the children can think about, discuss, and record what they are likely to see, which questions they may be able to investigate, whom they may talk to, and what they might bring back to the classroom. Fieldwork may not necessitate leaving the school but usually involves leaving the classroom to investigate some aspect of the environment more closely.

There is a lot to study on the way to and from the site.

Field Visit The class can go to a site that affords opportunities to see relevant objects, plants, animals, vehicles, events, equipment, people, and processes. The children take field notes and make sketches of what they are most interested in and what they would most like to learn more about when they return to school. The visit may not require special transportation if it is within walking distance. There is usually much of interest to study on the way to the site.

Fieldwork Follow-up The children discuss the field visit and record what happened, whom they spoke to, what they saw, and what they learned. Sketches made in the field become the basis for detailed drawings or paintings and for the construction of models. Secondary sources of information are consulted: encyclopedias, books, CDs, and the Internet. New questions are raised and letters written. Sometimes a follow-up field trip is planned.

Visiting Experts These are people who have firsthand experience of the topic being studied, through their work, travel, or leisure pursuits. Visiting experts can be invited to the classroom to talk to the children and answer questions.

Phase 3 ~ Concluding the Project

Debriefing A culminating event can be arranged that involves communicating, sharing, and presenting the work of the project to others who may be interested. This provides an excellent opportunity to review and evaluate all that has been going on during the past days or weeks. Usually there is too much to share everything, so the class has to be selective in deciding what would best tell the story of their study.

Personalizing New Knowledge Some children need time to reflect on new knowledge in order to understand it fully in their own terms. Children vary very much in this regard. Imaginative activity is helpful for many children: They make up their own stories and dramatic sequences to play out some of the new ideas. Children's literature can be especially helpful for this process of making the information personally memorable.

HOW DO CHILDREN DEMONSTRATE UNDERSTANDING?

The teacher ensures that all children are involved in various kinds of work in each of the three phases. Children apply their skills in representing their understanding as it is at first, as it develops, and as they find it particularly memorable for themselves. Throughout the project they draw, discuss, dramatize, write, collect data, measure, calculate, predict, diagram, record observations, read for information and pleasure, compose music and sing songs, and many other things. Each of the phases of the project offers its own special sources of inspiration and interest to energize the work.

Children each depict their understanding in unique ways.

During Each Phase

Phase 1 The children recall past experience and represent memories of relevant events, objects, and people.

Phase 2 The children have new experiences and investigate, draw from observation, construct models, observe closely and record findings, explore, predict, experiment and invent, and discuss and dramatize. It is mainly in this phase that longer-term, multistage project work is undertaken.

Phase 3 The children review and summarize the work they have done and recreate it in a new form to show another audience what they have achieved as a class. They also do more imaginative work, representing new information acquired in Phase 2 in original and personal ways.

PHASE 1
Starting the Project

TEACHER'S CONCERNS

- What relevant experiences have the children already had?
- What do the children already know?
- What can the children learn from each other?
- What questions are they asking?
- What misconceptions (if any) have been expressed?
- How can parents be involved with the work?

KEY EVENTS

- Initial discussion of the topic
- Story, video, or object to study, discuss, and speculate about
- Topic web of current knowledge — baseline of class understanding
- List of questions to find out about

CHILDREN'S WORK

- Recall personal experiences
- Represent personal memories
- Discuss and compare common and different experiences
- Brainstorm current knowledge and ideas
- Formulate personal questions

PHASE 2	PHASE 3
Investigation and Representation	**Concluding the Project**
• What new firsthand experiences can the children be given? • What new understanding can they acquire? • What fieldwork can be arranged? • How can curriculum goals best be met? • How can the work be diversified to accommodate individual learning needs and interests?	• What kind of culminating event would be most appropriate for this project? • What kinds of imaginative activity would best enable these children to personalize their recently acquired knowledge? • What kinds of main understandings should be consolidated, and how?
• Preparing for the field trip • Fieldwork: making sketches and field notes on site • Follow-up work: elaborating the sketches, writing and illustrating reports • Library research • Interviewing experts	• Culminating event • Personalizing new knowledge
• Preparatory discussion before field trip • Fieldwork • Secondary source research • Follow-up discussion and plans to represent what was learned • Visiting experts • Long-term, multistage work	• Reviewing all the work accomplished on the project • Evaluating work and deciding on the best and most representative pieces • Recreating the project learning so that others appreciate the story • Imaginative work and fantasy in art, writing, and literature • Selecting the work for the school records and work to take home

Children's Work: Process and Products

What do projects look like from the learner's point of view? Projects provide children with developmentally appropriate goals while offering teachers a foundation for understanding children's progress.

In project work children will mostly be applying skills in which they already have some fluency. Some activities may be simple one-time events, like painting a picture or writing a letter. Other activities may require more planning, like conducting a survey, collecting data, organizing it, and representing it in a bar graph. Some activities may be quite open-ended and evolve through several stages, such as constructing a model town. This may require research into architecture, building construction, scale measurement, and designing the layout, depending on the age of the children. Where several children are involved in such a venture, they have to discuss the progress of the work and share the tasks involved. Occasionally, children may decide to undertake the preparation of a book. For a young child, making a book may be quite a simple process. For an older child, such work might take several weeks and require extensive research, work on text and illustrations, several pilot drafts, and the ultimate creation of an appropriate index.

WHAT IS THE PROCESS OF WORKING ON PROJECTS?

As children do more project work, they become familiar with this process framework of planning, developing, and concluding a piece of work. They can see its applicability to many different kinds of enterprise. Once children commit themselves to a task, over time they become very involved and motivated to finish it to their personal satisfaction. It is important, of course, to help them be realistic in their aspirations and plans, but it is surprising how inventive they can be with the help of teacher, peers, and parents as the work progresses.

All multistage work entails a similar three-part framework of design and planning, implementation and development, and final draft and presentation/ publication.

Quality in Different Kinds of Work Product

In order to provide children with more detailed self-assessment criteria, each part of the framework can be further subdivided.

❶ Design and planning:
   a. initial idea
   b. planning

❷ Implementation and development:
   c. doing and recording development
   d. discussion

❸ Concluding the work:
   e. final draft
   f. sharing with the class

Note: c and d are recursive processes and do not necessarily follow in sequence.

Three Case Studies The three examples described here are typical of the kind of work that can be done in a class project on some aspect of the rural environment. One boy is constructing a model tractor following a visit to a farm. A group of eight children decide to edit and publish a class newspaper with a format similar to the one produced in the rural community they are studying. Two girls decide to make their own books about creatures they observed on the visit to the farm.

In the first example, the child is working on his own. In the second, the children are collaborating in quite a large group and will need considerable support from the teacher. The two girls in the third example are working in parallel, sharing ideas but working on separate products.

CASE STUDY EXAMPLES

An analysis of a Grade 5 project on the rural community and environment.

Stages	Making a Model Tractor
Design and Planning	Adam sketches a tractor while on a field trip to a farm. On return to the classroom, he decides to make a model and looks at his sketch for the details. He writes a list of materials to collect for the construction.
Implementation & Development	Adam sorts the materials he has collected into items suitable for the different parts of the tractor. The wheels in his sketch do not give him precise enough information for the model, so he gets a library book on farm vehicles and implements. He measures proportions and takes notes. He builds the parts and joins them together. He is helped with suggestions from a friend and the teacher about the structure and function of the tractor chassis.
Concluding the Work	The finishing touches on Adam's model involve further research as the details have to be painted in, spokes added to the wheels, door handles put on, etc. Adam makes a stand to display the finished model and a notice to go with it. He also makes labels for the parts. He links these to the model with pieces of thread. He writes a small booklet on "How I Made This Tractor." He also contributes an article to the class newspaper on the importance of tractors in running a farm.

Class Newspaper	Writing a Book
A class discussion suggests the creation of an editorial board. Roles: reporter, advice columnist, health and safety-advice editor, letter editor, illustrator, photographer, etc. The group arranges to collect and study the local newspaper for ideas about the different parts.	Amy chooses to write a book about snails, and her friend Eva one about spiders. They are keeping both kinds of animal in the class terrarium. They write down what they already know about their creatures and some questions they would like to research for the books.
The children cut up the newspapers and study the different parts. They see how the life of their classroom could be reported on and the members of their community served by a newspaper. Jerome takes pictures of the work in progress to report on the week's work. Chris interviews students and the teacher. Jane invites letters for the advice column and Peter for the Healthy Hints! column. Doug invites classmates to write letters to the paper.	The girls list characteristics of living things they recall from last year. They get a library book and compare their list with the table in the book. They decide on titles, how to organize the contents, what they will write about, and what illustrations to have. They do some observational research at the vivarium, taking notes on what the snails and spiders do. They find further information in books. They write about feeding, reproduction, males and females, etc.
Considerable industry and limited finesse accompany the first edition. But once it is out children can see its potential and contribute ideas for improvement. Genna collected the files and took them home to seek her mother's advice on the final layout. The next day all the parts were assembled with the pictures. The paper was positioned where one or two children at a time could read it. A suggestions box was set up for comments.	Amy and Eva have finished the main body of the text and illustrations of their books. They survey friends to see which parts of the books most interest them. This gives them an idea of which words to list in the index. They also list the books they consulted. They make the cover and work with a parent volunteer on book binding. The completed books look inviting. They are put on display in the book corner. Book reviews are commissioned by a Class 6H Journal editor.

HOW ARE SKILLS AND CONTENT ADDRESSED?

It is helpful to consider both the processes and the products of project work in relation to the curriculum subjects and basic skills. For example, project work in:

- language arts may include listening and speaking in discussions, cooperative-learning activities, and dramatic role-play. Children can also read and engage in many different forms of writing.
- mathematics may include frequency data presented in bar graphs, proportional data in pie charts, and measurements and calculations in written accounts of investigations.
- social studies may include surveys, maps, timelines, sequence charts, library research, and interviews with experts.
- science may include reports of explorations, investigations, experiments, and inventions.
- art may include drawings, paintings, printing, sculpture, and modeling.
- music may involve the students in writing their own songs and planning, rehearsing, and performing their own informal concerts.

Reading Instruction Can Easily Be Incorporated Into Project Work.
Reading should be a big part of children's project work. Books can be provided for research by the children themselves for the project activities they are engaged in. Sets of informative books can be borrowed from the school or public library for use in the classroom for the duration of the project. Such book selections may be restricted, but access to the library can also be arranged with the help of the librarian or aides and volunteers.

Reading expository texts will help children become writers of reports and essays.

In addition to reading for information, children can be encouraged to read stories and poems related to the topic for pleasure.

Activities for Younger Children For younger children (K–3), it may be more helpful to think of three broad categories of activity: dramatic play, construction, and investigation. These children may need more support from the teacher when they undertake the more complex and multistage activities which can be listed under these headings.

❶ Investigation

Support for investigation can take the following forms:

- encouraging free play and exploration with new materials
- encouraging much discussion of ideas
- suggesting and eliciting questions for exploration
- offering alternative ways to record findings

❷ Construction

Support for construction can take the following forms:

- suitable furnishing of an area in the room
- provision of a variety of equipment and materials
- protective clothing
- establishing routines for work preparation and cleaning up
- suggesting strategies to encourage exploration of alternative solutions to problems
- peer consulting and collaboration

❸ Dramatic Play

Support for role-play can take the following forms:

- screening and furnishing an area in the classroom for such activity
- providing props to stimulate play and discussion
- suggesting ideas from time to time to support and elaborate the play
- offering opportunities for short performances

PRODUCTS OF PROJECT WORK

Products of children's work can take many forms: single pages of writing or drawing, constructions, informal books, or dramatic performances. The children take great pride in the finished product of a sequence of tasks undertaken over several days and they also appreciate and learn from each other's finished work. Finished products are also much appreciated by parents, who want to see the results of the children's efforts in their project work. Finally, they provide opportunities for the teacher and child to discuss the quality of the work done.

CHILDREN'S WORK AT THE SIX STAGES

These are descriptions of the stages of the children's work in Phase 2, Investigation and Representation. At each of the stages there are questions to be considered, problems to be solved, or tasks to be achieved.

	Stages	Surveys on Shopping in a Local Mall
Design and Planning	**INITIAL IDEA**	Decide on a topic, such as a population of people, a sample, and questions to investigate. e.g., How many shoppers live near the mall? Which stores do they use most? Which stores do they like best for service?
	PLANNING	Three children each plan to ask the three questions of 12 people. They plan to use tallies to collect the data and take field notes.
Implementation & Development	**DOING & RECORDING**	The children begin to carry out their plan on the field visit with the class. They do not finish. They tidy up the data they have collected but need more.
	DISCUSSION	They decide to enlist the help of friends who live near the mall. Six of their friends agree to help. They finally get data on 24 people and decide that they have done enough to write an interesting report.
Concluding the Work	**FINAL PRODUCT**	Careful presentation, clearly printed titles, correctly labeled axes, and writing to explain the information in the graph are completed.
	SHARING	The children explain their original idea to the class. They describe their plans, the problems, and the help of friends. They explain the graphs and their report.

Investigating Birds Feeding	Mural and Wall Display
Students would like to know which birds come to the class bird feeder and which foods they prefer. They want to investigate the birds' feeding habits.	Students want to create a large mural representing the water cycle (ideas on the use and misuse of water are included). This mural will become the background for the work commissioned from other classmates.
The students plan to place food of several kinds on the bird feeder, observe for periods of 10 minutes at a time, and make likely predictions.	The students discuss their plans with selected friends and ask for volunteers. They plan a sketch of the background mural, keeping in mind the amount of wall space available.
Since the students realize that the birds may not come during their scheduled observations, they decide to measure the food's disappearance. They also ask their classmates to alert them to bird sightings.	The students paint the mural. They collect their classmates' work. There are reports and charts on irrigation of crops, on drinking water, water treatment plants, and so on.
Some students suggest other ways to estimate birds' feeding preferences. Other classmates agree to help out by taking part in the survey of bird sightings.	The students discuss the dimensions of the work collected and decide with the authors where their contribution might best be displayed over the mural (most logical, most aesthetically pleasing, etc.).
Students write an investigation report that includes pictures of the bird table, charts of the kinds of food, and a graph of the different types of birds seen.	The display is complete. There are charts, diagrams, graphs, and maps. There are scale models of machinery. There is a great deal of writing on the topic.
They present their investigation and findings to the whole class. There is some discussion of the validity of the results. The final report is made available for reading.	The class gathers around the display. The group presents their project, including the problems they had and how they were solved. They thank the contributors who presented their work.

Evaluation and Assessment

Authentic performance assessment and evaluation become the means to systematically document children's development. Documentation is critical to this process. Systematic instruction and project work involve different kinds of opportunity for assessment.

Systematic instruction provides the teacher with evidence of what the child is able to do when he is working at the edge of his capability. Project work offers different assessment opportunities: It shows the teacher what the child is capable of when he is working at the independent level, when he is applying the skills he already has in situations that are meaningful for him. Project work allows the teacher to assess the ability of the child to apply the skills he has. It enables the teacher to learn about the child as a person and to engage in progressive and meaningful dialogue on a range of issues.

Projects provide opportunities for performance-based assessment. What evidence of learning should teachers collect? What should they do with the information?

Systematic instruction shows

- how the child is acquiring skills

- the pace of learning

- the response to instruction

- areas of learning difficulties

- the effectiveness of practice tasks

Project work shows

- how the child is applying skills

- whether the child understands when to use skills

- the child's approach to work

- the depth of the child's understanding

- how resourceful the child is in the solution of problems

- how well the child is able to collaborate with others in the pursuit of common goals

WHEN SHOULD EVALUATION TAKE PLACE?

The teacher is constantly learning about the children in the classroom. Every decision a teacher makes, however small, involves a judgment. These judgments are based on careful observation, questioning of children, and a clear sense of what ought to be happening in the classroom if children are learning effectively.

Each of the three stages can provide a useful basis for evaluation and assessment. They are restated below with some questions a teacher can ask herself as she assesses the quality of children's work.

Initial Idea

• What is its potential for the child's learning?

• How clear is it?

• What is the scale of the idea? (too big or too small)

• How complex is it, and what resources will be needed?

• How original and imaginative is it?

• How appropriate for this project?

Planning

• What sequence of stages will the work progress through?

• How detailed is the list of resources required?

• How clear an idea has the child of the work involved?

• How detailed are the sketches (drawings) in the plans?

• What research does the child anticipate doing?

• How well suited to the child's ability are the plans?

Doing and Recording

• How does the work progress?

• What questions are raised?

• What research is done, in books or through consultation?

• How are research findings incorporated into the work?

• How is the progress of the work being recorded?

• How is the child applying basic academic skills in this work?

Discussion

• What is the purpose of the discussion engaged in? (decision-making? exploration of ideas? consultation? advice?)
• How focused is it?
• What decisions are made on the basis of the discussion?
• How are the results of discussion recorded and/or implemented?

Final Product

• How does the final product reflect the original planning?
• How clearly are the ideas presented?
• How imaginative and original are the ideas incorporated in it?
• How does it reflect the development of the child's thinking?

RECORD-KEEPING

The original planning web made by the teacher (and children, if older) can provide a basis for recording the progress made by the class throughout the project. Using a color coding (different color for each week), the teacher can mark the areas studied. Children's names can be included. Levels of depth or elaboration (high interest), changes of direction, and undeveloped (low interest) areas can all be recorded on the original web.

For any kind of assessment it is important for the teacher to keep records. Assessment records show how progress is being made by each child over time. The comparison of similar work done several weeks or months apart can give a good idea of which aspects of skill and understanding are improving and which need further development.

The project work itself results in finished products that represent the child's achievement at the point at which the work was completed. Samples of project work can be annotated by the teacher and kept in a personal portfolio of work for each child. The children can also collect project work in a project folder of their own. At the end of the project each child and the teacher together can select pieces of work for the portfolio. The rest of the work in the project folder can be taken home for the family to keep.

The teacher can keep a record of every activity undertaken during the project and the date when each child completed the work he or she elected to do. In this way the teacher can keep an account of each child's achievements for reference. Records of achievement are important for conferences with parents and for passing on to the teacher who will be teaching the child the next year.

The Roles of Teachers, Students, and Parents

How is a community of collaboration and contribution created? Learning incorporates not only teachers and children but parents as well. Involving parents in the project allows for the continuity of experience between home and school.

Children have learned how to learn with their parents at home before they ever come to school. The language they use at home can help them in school. School learning is of a rather different type; especially different is the language of systematic instruction.

Project work, however, offers intensive work and learning opportunities conducted in a language that can be more easily understood at home. Projects are about the real world. The topics most often build on children's firsthand experience. The children can be encouraged to find things out by talking to their parents. They do not need talk about abstruse and technical things but about shops, vehicles, travel, holidays, where food comes from, where the water goes down the drain, and what the world was like when their parents were children.

There was a time, a hundred years ago or more, when children knew a great deal more about the life support systems in their lives. In these days of electricity and automation, the world is a much more magic place for children. Parents find it difficult to answer young children's questions about the real world because the answers are too complicated for them to understand. As a result, children tend not to be as fluent in their understanding of everyday cause and effect as they once were.

With parents to help bridge the gap between life in school and life at home, teachers can help children to understand how things work, where things come from, how they get made or fixed, and who knows about these things. A project on household water, for instance, can draw together those children whose parents have some understanding of how the plumbing in their home works. Maybe one of the parents is a plumber — or has a friend who is—and could come to school, show tools and equipment, and talk about his or her work.

The kind of work described above, which children do in the course of projects, is about complex content that parents can understand and relate to. The children apply the skills the parents are most concerned about as they pursue their study. As they work, the children become interested in the kinds of everyday things their parents can help them understand. This is empowering to parents who wish to support their child's education, and it encourages children to seek and appreciate their parents' help, experience, and advice.

The role of both the teacher and parents is to listen, observe, ask questions, reflect, and provoke.

Parents can become interested and involved in project work alongside their children. They can come to school as volunteers and work with groups or individual children as they undertake independent study. The teacher can help them understand what might be most useful in the classroom in the way of help, support, and encouragement to children.

Where rich and productive project work is going on alongside systematic instruction in basic skills, schools become places where children learn willingly, parents support their learning, and teachers enjoy the challenge of life in the classroom.

Conclusion

Final Words

This practical guide has been written to enable teachers to introduce the Project Approach into teaching and learning in the elementary classroom. In junior high school, the approach can be adapted to meet the needs of older children and their teachers.

There is a general concern among educators about how to best effect education improvement. It is hoped that teachers can use this political and professional climate to develop their own teaching in such a way that they feel happier about what they are doing in their own classrooms.

The most important people in the education system are the teachers and the children. They work day by day in classrooms separated from the outside world. If changes are to occur in the way teachers teach, the way children learn in school, and the way parents understand how their children can learn most effectively, then the place to start is in the classroom. Teachers need to work together with the children who are their responsibility and the parents who can provide such influential support of their children's learning.

This guide to the Project Approach has been written with teachers in mind. The examples are genuine ones. The author and many others teach children this way. The approach reflects the experience of teachers from different countries and in different stages of professional development.

It is better to start small. I would recommend only one or two hours a week, perhaps, where the children are working quite differently from the rest of the time. This gives the teacher a chance to get used to the workshop atmosphere and to evaluate with the children the advantages of working this way. Once any initial difficulties have been ironed out and the children are enthusiastic about their work, the teacher can plan for the approach to take over one or two complete afternoons a week. If this works well it will soon be possible to extend the project work into the rest of the time and try systematic instruction of small groups alongside the project work.

The author has studied the work of teachers, listened to their concerns, and conducted many workshops on the Project Approach in Canada and the U.S.A. It is an approach rather than a method to be followed in its entirety. It suggests a number of ways to empower children and teachers to take initiative in the classroom. By such means, both teachers and children can be challenged to learn and achieve at high levels with interest and determination.

There is much still to learn about how teachers adapt their teaching to meet the individual needs of children in school. If you wish to share your own explorations of any strategies suggested in this guide, I would be very pleased to hear from you and to respond to any questions you may have about the Project Approach. It is hoped that teachers can find ideas here for their professional development that will help them to meet the challenges of the future with enhanced commitment and confidence.

RESOURCES

Katz, L. G. & Chard, S. C. *Engaging Children's Minds: The Project Approach.* New Jersey: Ablex Publishing, 1989.
Projects Web Site: http://www.ualberta.ca/~ schard/projects.htm

Teacher's Notes

PHASE 1 ~ STARTING THE PROJECT

Teacher's Notes

Teacher's Notes

PHASE 2 ~ INVESTIGATION AND REPRESENTATION

Teacher's Notes

Teacher's Notes

PHASE 3 ~ CONCLUDING THE PROJECT

Teacher's Notes